SOLOS

FOR THE

OBOE

PLAYER

With Piano Accompaniment

Selected and Edited by

WHITNEY TUSTIN

ED 2502
ISBN 978-0-7935-5421-8

G. SCHIRMER, Inc.

DISTRIBUTED BY
HAL•LEONARD®
CORPORATION
7777 W. BLUEMOUND RD. P.O. BOX 13819 MILWAUKEE, WI 53213

Note

Solos for the Oboe Player have been chosen with great care from the wealth of available material. The pieces offer the player a variety of periods and styles.

The piano accompaniments for the Telemann and Loeillet sonatas have been freely realized from the figured bass; this is also true of the Fasch, originally written for two oboes and continuo. Wagner's song, *Träume,* seems admirably suited to the oboe; and the theme from the slow movement of Bizet's *Symphony in C* is a charming solo in itself. The orchestral score has been transcribed for the piano.

The Liszt songs, Debussy's *Mazurka* and the Rachmaninoff and Berger vocalises have always seemed natural oboe pieces to me. They are here presented as an addition to the literature — transcribed with slight modifications to suit the instrument.

W.T.

CONTENTS

Index by Composers

1. Aria

from: St. Matthew Passion

JOHANN SEBASTIAN BACH (1685-1750)
Arranged by W.T.

45335 cx

2

2. Sonata in A Minor

I

GEORG PHILIPP TELEMANN (1681-1767)
Arranged by W.T.

II

III

8

IV

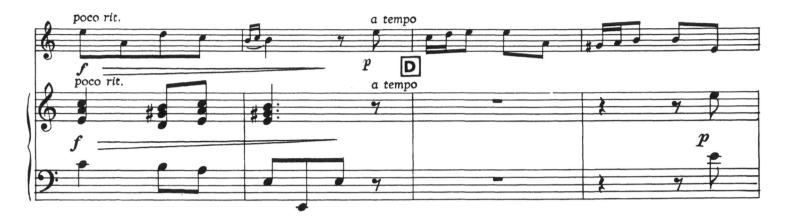

3. Largo

JOHANN FRIEDRICH FASCH (1688-1758)
Arranged by W.T.

4. Concerto No. 8 in B♭

GEORGE FRIDERIC HANDEL (1685-1759)
Arranged by W.T.

II

18

45335

III
Siciliana

45335

poco a poco cresc. poco a

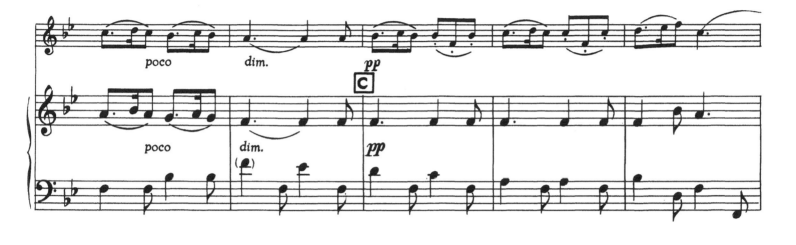

poco dim. **pp**

IV

23

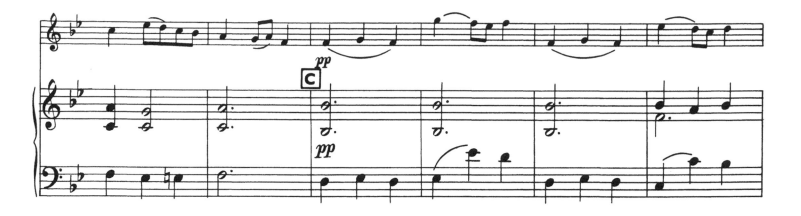

45335

5. Andante and Allegro

from: Sonata No. 15

JEAN-BAPTISTE LOEILLET (1680-1730)
Arranged by W.T.

26

45335

6. Romance No. 1

from: Three Romances

ROBERT SCHUMANN, Op. 94
(1810-1856)
Arranged by W.T.

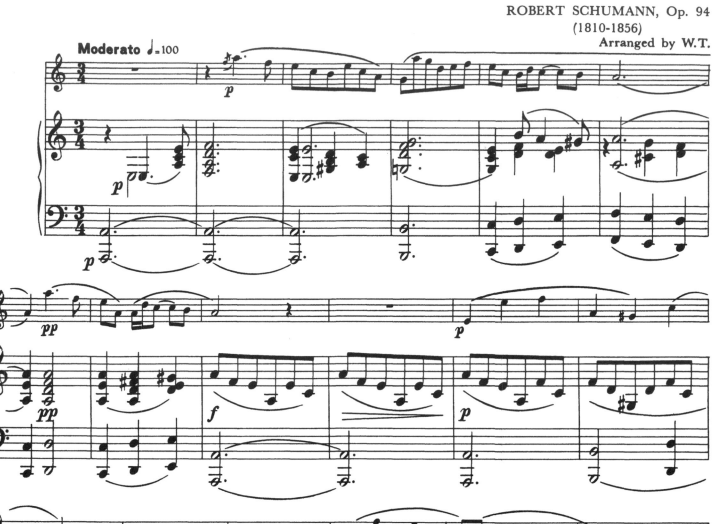

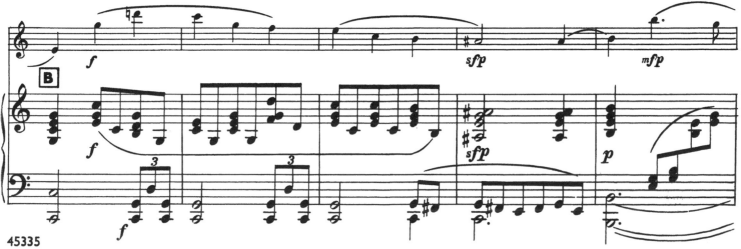

45335

SOLOS

FOR THE

OBOE

PLAYER

With Piano Accompaniment

Selected and Edited by

WHITNEY TUSTIN

OBOE

ED 2502
ISBN 978-0-7935-5421-8

G. SCHIRMER, Inc.

DISTRIBUTED BY

HAL•LEONARD®
CORPORATION

7777 W. BLUEMOUND RD. P.O. BOX 13819 MILWAUKEE, WI 53213

CONTENTS

		Piano	Oboe

The player should mark each selection with these cue markings for ease of use. To include as many selections as possible on the record, it was necessary to eliminate certain repeats. Listen to the record and mark the music accordingly before playing with the record.

1. Aria - J. S. Bach	Larghetto	5 taps plus 1 silent (1 measure) precede music.
2. Sonata in A minor - Telemann	Siciliana	4 taps (1 measure) precede music.
	Vivace	4 taps (2 measures) precede music. Piano enters on upbeat of 2nd beat in 2nd measure after letter D.
3. Largo - Fasch		8 taps (1 measure) precede music
4. Concerto #8 in Bb - Handel	Vivace	6 taps (2 measures) precede music.
5. Andante and Allegro - Loeillet	Andante	3 taps (1 measure) precede music.
6. Romance No. 1 - Schumann	Moderato	3 taps (1 measure) precede piano entrance.
12. Vocalise - Rachmaninoff		4 taps (1 measure) precede music.

1. Aria

from: St. Matthew Passion

OBOE

JOHANN SEBASTIAN BACH (1685-1750)
Arranged by W.T.

45335 cx

2. Sonata in A Minor

OBOE

I

GEORG PHILIPP TELEMANN (1681-1767)
Arranged by W. T.

II

III

4

IV

45335

OBOE

3. Largo

JOHANN FRIEDRICH FASCH (1688-1758)
Arranged by W.T.

45335

4. Concerto No. 8 in B♭

OBOE

GEORGE FRIDERIC HANDEL (1685-1759)
Arranged by W.T.

III
Siciliana

IV

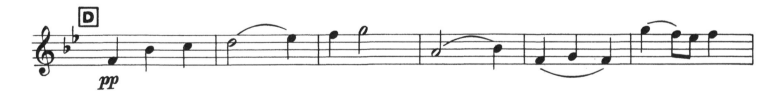

OBOE

5. Andante and Allegro

from: Sonata No. 15

JEAN-BAPTISTE LOEILLET (1680-1730)
Arranged by W.T.

45335

10

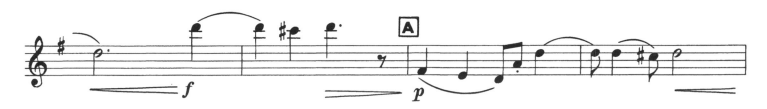

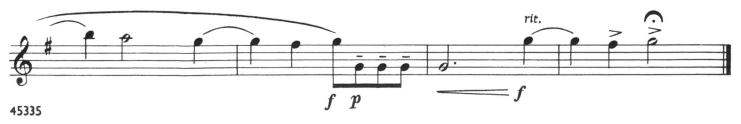

6. Romance No. 1

from: Three Romances

ROBERT SCHUMANN, Op. 94
(1810-1856)
Arranged by W.T.

OBOE

45335

7. Dreams

(Träume)

OBOE

RICHARD WAGNER (1813-1883)
Arranged by W.T.

OBOE

8. Two Songs

I

It must be wonderful, withal

FRANZ LISZT (1811-1886)
Arranged by W.T.

II

Joyful and Woeful

45335

9. Theme
from: Symphony in C, 2nd Movement

OBOE

GEORGES BIZET (1838-1875)
Arranged by W.T.

10. Two Arabian Dances

OBOE

I

MAX LAURISCHKUS, Op. 3
(1876-1929)
Arranged by W. T.

Andante con moto quasi allegretto ♪ = 144

45335

II

OBOE

11. Mazurka

CLAUDE DEBUSSY (1862-1918)
Arranged by W.T.

45335

12. Vocalise

OBOE

SERGEI RACHMANINOFF, Op. 34, No. 14
(1873-1943)
Arranged by W.T.

13. Song

from: Two Pieces

OBOE

REINHOLD GLIÈRE, Op. 35, No. 3
(1875-1956)
Arranged by W. T.

14. Kuruka-Kuruka

KÕSÇAK YAMADA (1886-   )
Arranged by W.T.

OBOE

15. Toadinha
(A Little Song)

OBOE

JEAN BERGER (1901-   )
Arranged by W.T.

22

45335

7. Dreams
(Träume)

RICHARD WAGNER (1813-1883)
Arranged by W.T.

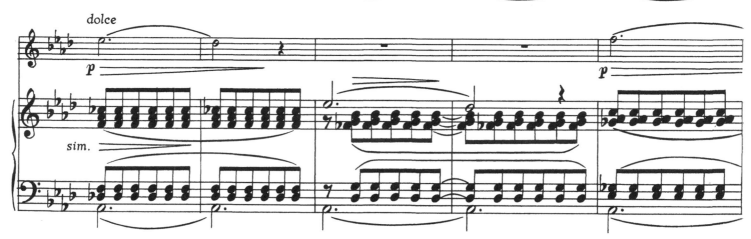

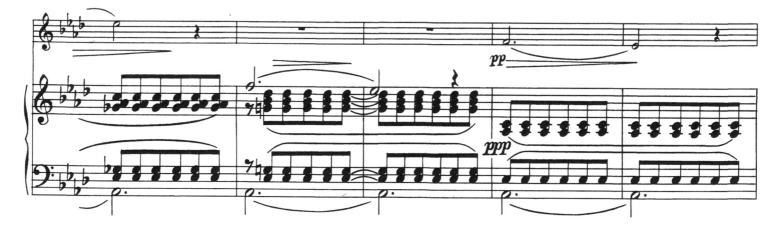

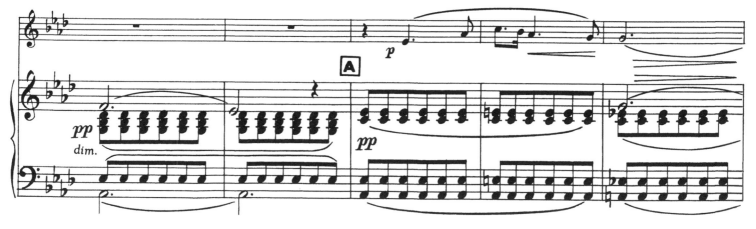

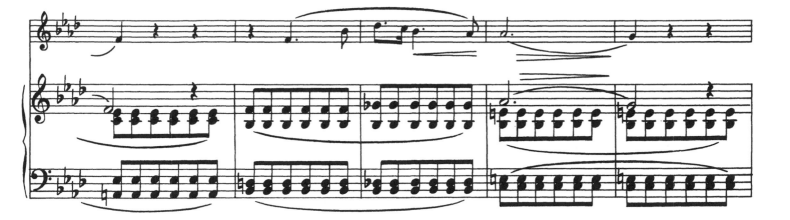

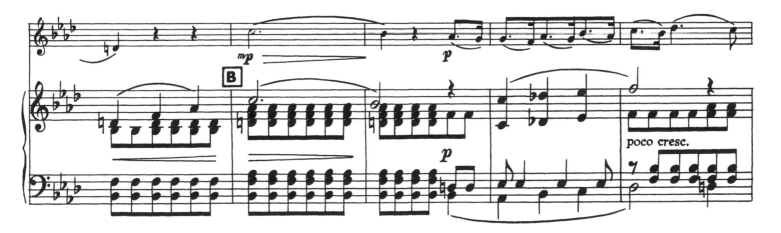

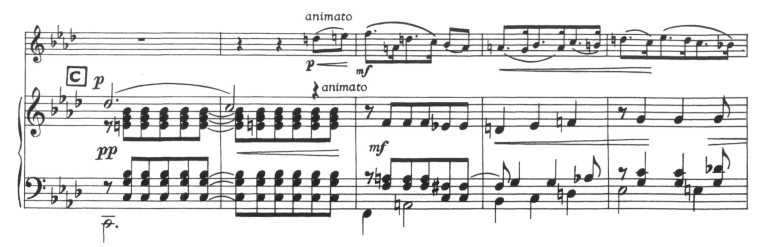

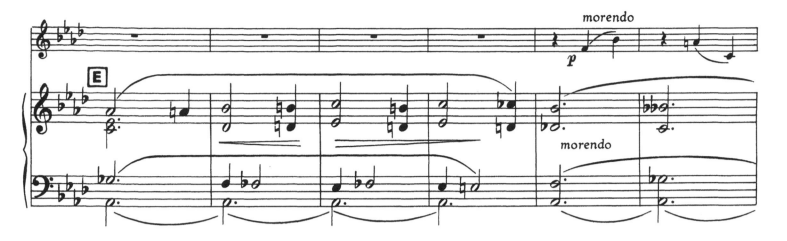

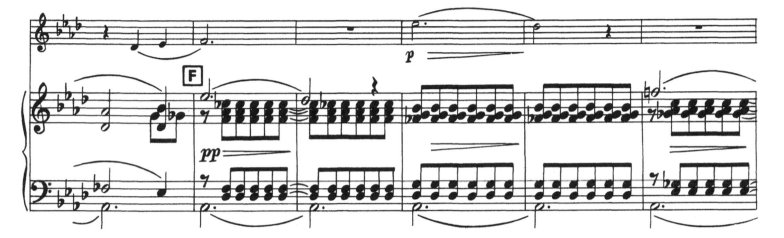

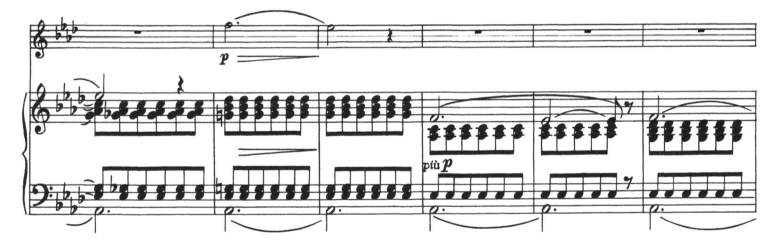

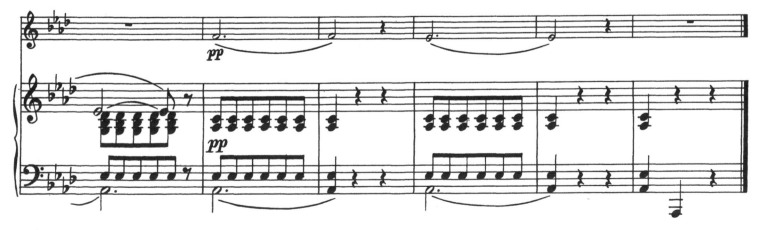

8. Two Songs

I

It must be wonderful, withal

FRANZ LISZT (1811-1886)
Arranged by W.T.

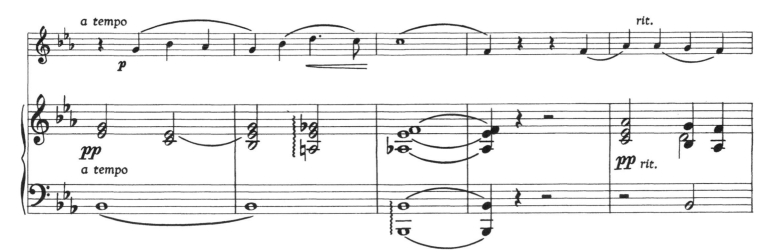

II
Joyful and woeful

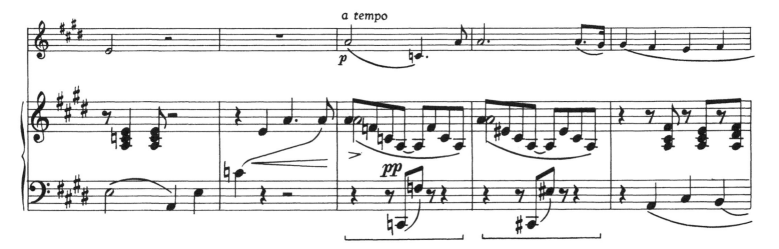

9. Theme

from: Symphony in C, 2nd Movement

GEORGES BIZET (1838-1875)
Arranged by W.T.

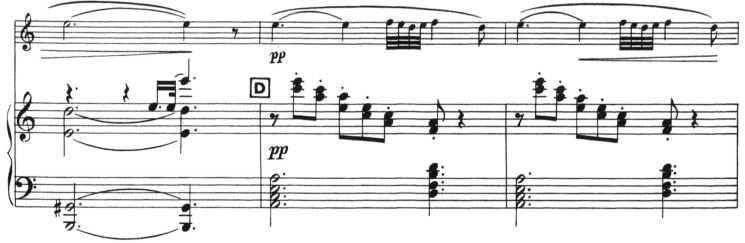

10. Two Arabian Dances

I

MAX LAURISCHKUS, Op. 3
(1876-1929)
Arranged by W.T.

Andante con moto, quasi allegretto ♪ = 144

II

45335

11. Mazurka

CLAUDE DEBUSSY (1862-1918)
Arranged by W.T.

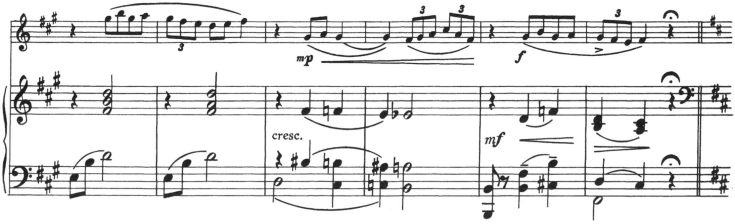

12. Vocalise

SERGEI RACHMANINOFF, Op. 34, No. 14
(1873-1943)
Arranged by W.T.

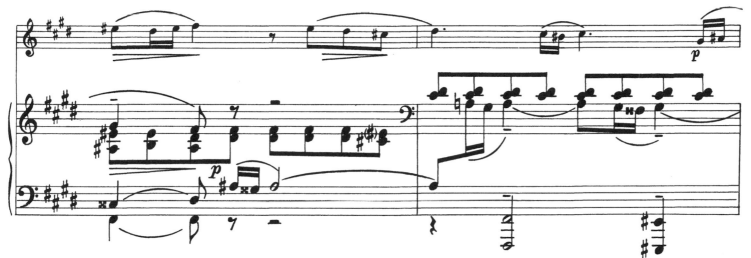

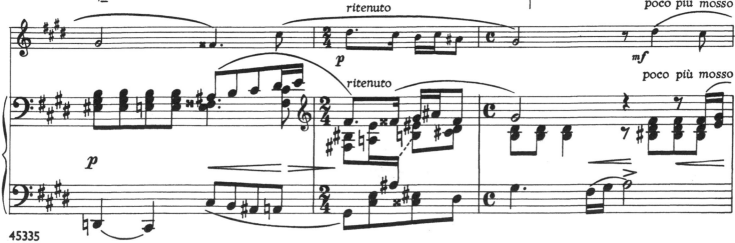

56

13. Song

from: Two Pieces

REINHOLD GLIÈRE, Op. 35, No. 3
(1875-1956)
Arranged by W.T.

45335

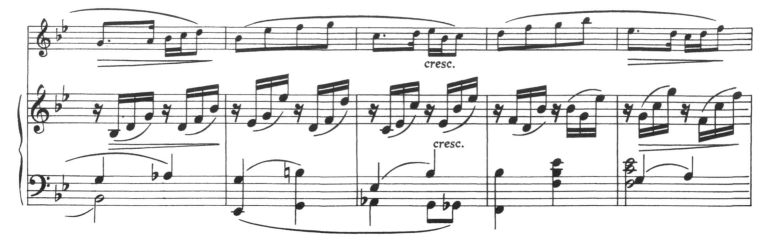

14. Kuruka-Kuruka

KŌSÇAK YAMADA (1886-   )
Arranged by W.T.

45335

15. Toadinha

(A Little Song)

JEAN BERGER (1901-   )
Arranged by W.T.

45335

64

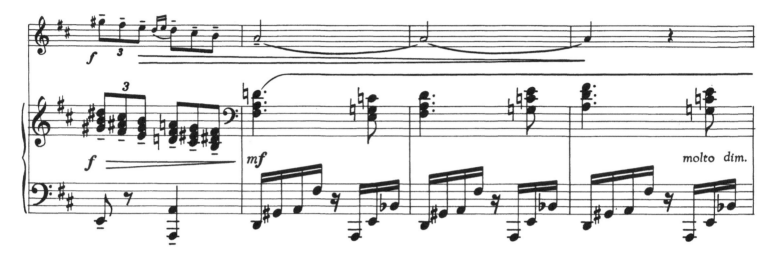

45335

45335

Molto più lento